CATS

by Laura French

illustrated by
Mel Crawford

A GOLDEN BOOK, New York
Western Publishing Company, Inc.
Racine, Wisconsin 53404

Chester and Rusty and Milo are cats. Like all cats —and just like people!—they are alike in some ways and very different in others.

Chester likes to take his naps on top of the TV set because it's so nice and warm.

Rusty knows where there's an open window at his house, and he can come and go whenever he wants to. Milo runs to the bedroom when he hears the alarm clock, to remind the people he lives with that it's time for breakfast.

All cats can hear and see especially well. Their ears
are set high on their heads, and they can move them
in many different directions to catch the faintest
little sounds.

On a sunny day, the black pupil at the center of a cat's eye is just a tiny slit. But in the dark, the pupil gets bigger and bigger, to let in as much light as possible. That's why your cat can see so much better in the dark than you can.

The long whiskers on the sides of a cat's face are important, too. They are "feelers" that tell the cat whether a space is wide enough for it to walk through.

Every cat has a coat of soft, warm fur. But the length and color of the coat help to make each cat look different.

Most cats have short fur. But some cats, like the
Persian, have long, thick, silky fur. Persian cats can
be almost any color—black, white, gray, or orange.

Persians have snub noses, wide faces, broad chests,
and short legs. They are quiet cats. They seem to
know that they are beautiful.

Siamese cats are very different from Persians. Their hair is short and rough. They have long, thin faces and long legs. Their bodies are creamy white, but their feet, tails, ears, and faces can be dark brown, gray, or even orange or pale blue.

Siamese cats seldom sit still for very long. Their long legs are perfect for jumping and running. Even grown-up Siamese play like kittens.

Siamese have loud, bossy voices, and they love to "talk" to people and to one another.

There are many other kinds of cats. Some of them are very unusual. The Rex cat has tightly curled fur—even its whiskers are kinky! The Manx cat is born without a tail. Himalayans have long fur, like Persians, but they have white bodies and dark faces, tails, feet, and ears, like Siamese.

Of course, even the common kinds of cats are beautiful. Tabby cats have gray or orange fur that is striped or swirled. Tortoiseshell cats have coats of orange, black, and cream, all mixed together. Calico cats have spots of those same colors on a background of white.

Other cats have some special marking that's all their own—a black patch around one eye, a white stocking, or a little spot of color between the ears.

All cats, long-haired or short-haired, Siamese or tabby, are tiny and helpless when they are born. Their eyes and ears are tightly closed to protect them from bright lights and loud noises. They stay close to their mother, who feeds them and keeps them warm and clean and safe from harm.

After about ten days, their eyes open, and they begin to look around and play.

All the while they are playing, kittens are practicing the things they will need to know as adults. The games of hide-and-seek teach them to hide from their enemies. By chasing a ball of yarn or a piece of string, they learn to hunt.

By the time a kitten is six weeks old, it has learned
to drink milk from a dish. Then it is old enough to
leave its mother. And in less than a year, it is able to
take care of itself very well indeed.

You can call a cat, but it won't come unless it wants to. You can pick a cat up, but it won't stay in your arms or on your lap unless it has decided—for itself—that it's time for a nap.

That's one of the things that cat lovers like best about cats—they are *independent*.

You can't teach a cat to do tricks, but if a cat lives in your house, it will learn tricks of its own, just as Chester and Rusty and Milo did.

Some cats learn to open cupboard doors or to turn on water faucets.

Many cats learn that there are good things to eat in the refrigerator, and they will come running when they hear its door open.

And every cat soon finds an especially comfortable place for stretching out to sleep.

Even though they are good at taking care of themselves, cats still must have help from the people they live with. To be healthy and happy, they need to be warm and dry. They need good food to eat and fresh water to drink.

If you take good care of the cat who lives in your house, it will thank you in its own ways. It will come to greet you when you get home, stretching and yawning as it wakes from a sound sleep. It will sit close to you, purring and stretching its neck so that you can scratch that certain place behind its ear or under its chin.

It will curl up at your feet when you settle down for the night. It will listen to secrets that you wouldn't tell anyone else.

The cat who lives in your house can be one of your very best friends.